Cambridge **Discovery Education**™

▶ **INTERACTIVE READERS**

Series editor: Bob Hastings

WHAT MAKES A PLACE SPECIAL?
MOSCOW, EGYPT, AUSTRALIA

A2

David Maule

CAMBRIDGE
UNIVERSITY PRESS

DISCOVERY
EDUCATION™

CAMBRIDGE UNIVERSITY PRESS
Cambridge, New York, Melbourne, Madrid, Cape Town,
Singapore, São Paulo, Delhi, Mexico City

Cambridge University Press
32 Avenue of the Americas, New York, NY 10013-2473, USA

www.cambridge.org
Information on this title: www.cambridge.org/9781107633179

First published 2014
Reprinted 2014

Printed in Hong Kong, China, by Golden Cup Printing Company Limited

A catalog record for this publication is available from the British Library.

Library of Congress Cataloging-in-Publication Data

Maule, David.
  What makes a place special? : Moscow, Egypt, Australia / David Maule.
     pages cm. -- (Cambridge discovery interactive readers)
  ISBN 978-1-107-63317-9 (pbk. : alk. paper)
1. Moscow (Russia)--Juvenile literature. 2. Egypt--Juvenile literature. 3. Australia--Juvenile
literature. 4. English language--Textbooks for foreign speakers. 5. Readers (Elementary) I. Title.

DK601.2.M33 2013
909--dc23

                              2013023919

ISBN 978-1-107-63317-9

Additional resources for this publication at www.cambridge.org

Layout services, art direction, book design, and photo research: Q2ABillSMITH GROUP
Editorial services: Hyphen S.A.
Audio production: CityVox, New York
Video production: Q2ABillSMITH GROUP

Contents

Before You Read:
Get Ready!

Here's a question. Think of Egypt. Now think of a building – something big. What do you see? Now think of a river – what's its name? Now think of something that is made in Egypt.

Think of one city, one country, or one continent. Can you name three things that describe it?

Words to Know

Look at the photos. Complete the information that follows with the words below the pictures.

war

fur

domes

Moscow is a city.

❶ It is famous for a kind of building. The tops look like onions! They are called onion _____ .

❷ It is very cold in winter in Moscow, so the people wear hats and coats made of _____ – the hair and skin of animals.

❸ There are monuments in Moscow to remember Russians who died in the Second World _____ .

Words to Know

Look at each set of photos. Complete the information that follows with the words below the pictures.

cotton   pyramids   flood

Egypt is a country in the north of Africa.

1 It is famous for its fantastic buildings – the _____ .

2 The river Nile goes through Egypt. In the past, farmers waited for the river to _____ every year to get water in their fields.

3 A lot of _____ is grown in Egypt. It is used to make clothes, bedsheets, pajamas, and other products.

marsupials   coral   Great Barrier Reef

Australia is a continent.

1 It is famous for the _____ – it is like a wall in the sea.

2 This beautiful world under the sea is made of _____ – animals that grow in warm water.

3 Australia is also famous for its animals on land, like kangaroos and koalas – they are _____ .

CHAPTER 1

City, Country, Continent

LET'S THINK ABOUT NEW YORK CITY. LET'S FIND THREE THINGS THAT SAY "NEW YORK!"

Think about a park, a food, and a way to travel around the city. Then answer the questions.

1 This park in New York is famous. You can see it in many movies. What's its name?
- Ⓐ Central Park
- Ⓑ Manhattan Park
- Ⓒ Brooklyn Park

2 Many people eat this type of bread for breakfast in New York. Sometimes they put meat or cheese on it. What is it?
- Ⓐ eggs
- Ⓑ bagel
- Ⓒ cake

3 In London, taxis are usually black. But New York taxis are a different color. What color are they?
- Ⓐ red
- Ⓑ blue
- Ⓒ yellow

Now let's think about the country of Italy. What do you think of? Buildings – maybe the Colosseum in Rome, or the Vatican? Food – pizza, pasta, ice cream? Other things – soccer, opera singing, the boats in Venice? Which three things would you choose to describe Italy?

An opera

Now let's look at **continents**. How many continents are there in the world? Most people say seven.

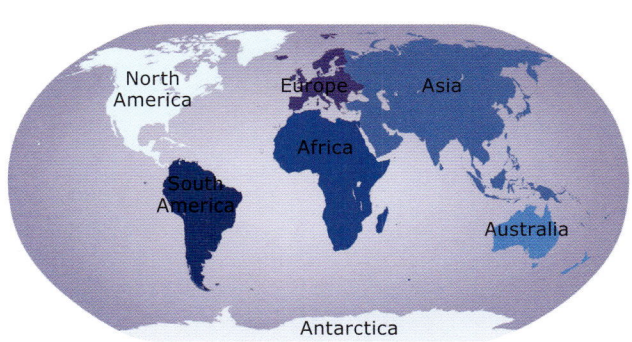

How good are you at geography?

1. Which continent has no countries?
2. It is the second largest continent. Which is it?
3. Three things: the Andes, Macchu Picchu, soccer. Which continent are you thinking about?

In this book we're going to look at a city, Moscow; a country, Egypt; and a continent, Australia.

For each of them, we're going to look at three things. These might be buildings, animals, people, types of food, or something else that people **connect** with that place.

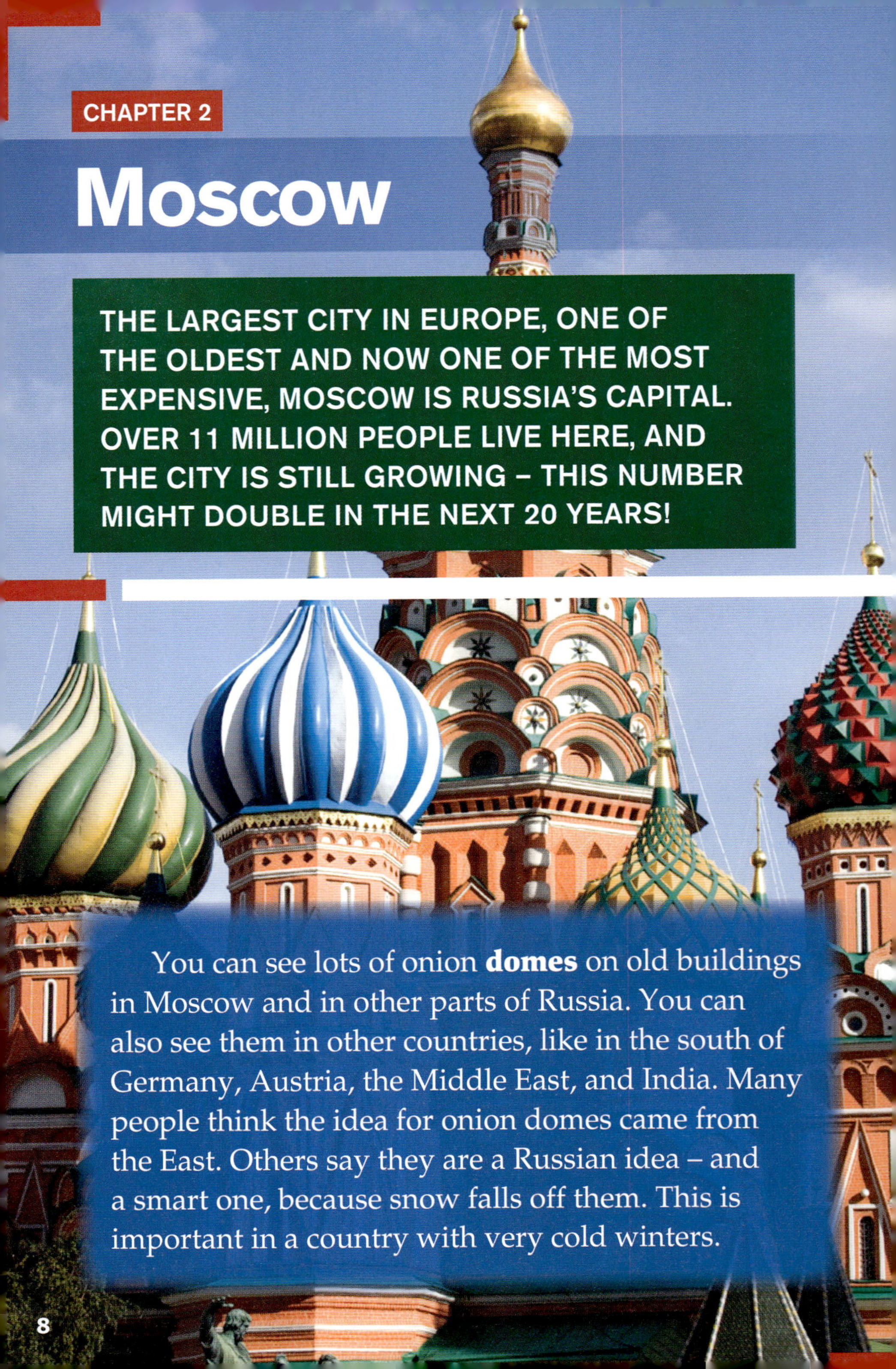

CHAPTER 2

MOSCOW

THE LARGEST CITY IN EUROPE, ONE OF
THE OLDEST AND NOW ONE OF THE MOST
EXPENSIVE, MOSCOW IS RUSSIA'S CAPITAL.
OVER 11 MILLION PEOPLE LIVE HERE, AND
THE CITY IS STILL GROWING – THIS NUMBER
MIGHT DOUBLE IN THE NEXT 20 YEARS!

You can see lots of onion **domes** on old buildings
in Moscow and in other parts of Russia. You can
also see them in other countries, like in the south of
Germany, Austria, the Middle East, and India. Many
people think the idea for onion domes came from
the East. Others say they are a Russian idea – and
a smart one, because snow falls off them. This is
important in a country with very cold winters.

This is Red Square, in the center of Moscow. On the right is St Basil's Cathedral with its onion domes. On the left is the Kremlin. In Russian, *kremlin* means "fortress."[1] Hundreds of years ago people hid in the Kremlin in times of danger. But today, visitors come to see its palaces,[2] its museums, and its four cathedrals.

In Moscow there are many old buildings, but there are many new buildings, too. It's a fast-growing city. People say that there are too many cars and it's very expensive to live there. But many people like living in Moscow because of the interesting shops and the nightlife.

[1] **fortress:** a kind of strong castle
[2] **palace:** a large house where a king or queen lives

Video Quest

Moscow

Watch this video to learn about **communism** in Russia. When did communism end there?

МОЛЛИ ГВИНН

In November 1939, the Soviet Union went to war with Finland. The war went on until the following March, so it's called the Winter War. Because their clothes weren't warm enough, many Soviet soldiers died from the cold. After the Winter War they got new winter clothes, and a special hat – the *ushanka*. Soviet soldiers wore these warm **fur** hats through the Second World War, or World War II.

After World War II ended in 1945, people in other countries started to wear ushankas because they're comfortable and warm, and they look good. They became popular in some northern European countries, and in Canada and the United States. The police and soldiers often wear them – and in the United States so do the people who bring the mail.

Many years ago people made ushankas from animal fur. Now they make the "fur" in factories. This is cheaper and stronger. Also, many people today don't want to kill animals to make hats.

Caviar is made from the eggs of the sturgeon fish.

This much caviar costs about $40. Enjoy!

Think of food in Russia. Think of something really expensive – maybe $10,000 a kilogram! At that price, you don't get much caviar for $40.

In the past, most caviar came from the rivers of Russia. Today, most caviar comes from the Caspian Sea, and most of that comes from Iran, not Russia. However, caviar also comes from the United States, Canada, and Saudi Arabia.

In 2012 there was a caviar-eating competition in a Moscow restaurant. The winner, Alexander Valov, ate $5,000 of caviar in less than a minute and a half. He won $340 – and some more caviar to take home.

? EVALUATE

People spend a lot of money on caviar and other expensive foods. Why? Do you think they taste better? What is the most expensive food you ever ate?

CHAPTER 3

Egypt

THINK OF THE WORLD'S LONGEST RIVER, THE NILE, AND YOU THINK OF EGYPT. BUT ONLY ABOUT TWENTY PERCENT OF ITS 6,719 KILOMETERS GO THROUGH EGYPT. LOOK AT THE MAP TO FIND THE OTHER EIGHT COUNTRIES THE NILE GOES THROUGH.

Heavy rains fall in some countries along the Nile, especially Ethiopia, during part of the year. For thousands of years this water went down to Egypt and flooded the fields. This was good for the farmers. They grew wheat,[3] fruits, and vegetables.

In 1968 Egypt began to build the Aswan **Dam** across the Nile River. This dam stops the flooding, but Egypt can still get the water it needs. During the times of heavy rains, the dam holds the water until it is needed later.

[3]**wheat:** a plant used for making bread

The pyramids at Giza

Thanks to the Nile, the Ancient[4] Egyptians had lots of food. They were rich. So they built fine buildings for the living and the dead. When pharaohs[5] died in Egypt, the people put their bodies inside pyramids. Everyone knows the famous pyramids at Giza, near Cairo. But did you know there are around 150 pyramids in Egypt?

Most of these pyramids are west of the Nile. This is because the sun goes down in the west, so people believed it was the land of the dead.

In the pyramids they put things that the dead pharaohs would need in their next life: food, plates, tables, chairs, money. But soon after the pharaohs were put in the pyramids, robbers broke into the pyramids and stole many of these things.

[4]**ancient:** from a very long time ago
[5]**pharaoh:** a king or queen in Egypt

Video Quest

Luxor

Watch this video about the city of Luxor in Egypt. Which is older, Luxor or the pyramids?

Cotton

Cotton grew along the Nile in Ancient Egypt, but in 1820 a Frenchman named Jumel found a new kind of cotton in a garden in Cairo. Jumel knew it was very good, so he showed it to Mehemet Ali, the ruler of Egypt at that time and the man who made Egypt a modern country. Ali told farmers to plant it all over southern Egypt. It grew well, and Egypt became famous for very fine cotton.

By the middle of the 1800s a lot of cotton was grown in the southern United States. American cotton was cheap, and so it was popular in Europe. However, when the United States Civil War started in 1861, they stopped selling American cotton. So Europeans bought Egyptian cotton instead, and its price went up and up.

Money came into Egypt. The people built big new streets, like those in Paris. Cairo got the name of "Paris on the Nile." However, in 1865 the war in the United States ended. This was good for the Americans, but not so good for the Egyptians. The price of cotton fell, and Egypt lost a lot of money.

Today cotton is not so important to Egypt. The country makes more money from gas and from its fruit, rice, and cheese. But people still like cotton from Egypt. The best Egyptian cotton is very soft and strong. It's easy to know if the cotton you buy is really from Egypt. Egyptian cotton always has a picture on it – it shows a cotton flower inside a pyramid.

ANALYZE

We use cotton for some of our clothes. What other things do we make clothes from? Do they come from plants or animals, or from plastic?

CHAPTER 4

Australia

THE LARGE ISLAND OF NEW GUINEA IS A COUNTRY TO THE NORTH OF AUSTRALIA. BUT IT'S ALSO IN AUSTRALIA! NEW GUINEA AND HUNDREDS OF OTHER SMALLER ISLANDS ARE PART OF THE CONTINENT OF AUSTRALIA.

Australia is the world's smallest continent, but the country of Australia is the sixth largest in the world. The first Europeans to live there came from Britain and Ireland. Australia is on the other side of the world from these countries, so that's why they call it Down Under. Since the 1900s, people from many countries have come to live in Australia: Italians, Greeks, Chinese, and Indians. But they all speak English.

The two largest cities in Australia are Sydney and Melbourne. They couldn't agree which should be the capital city, so they built a new city between them. This is Canberra. It became the capital in 1927.

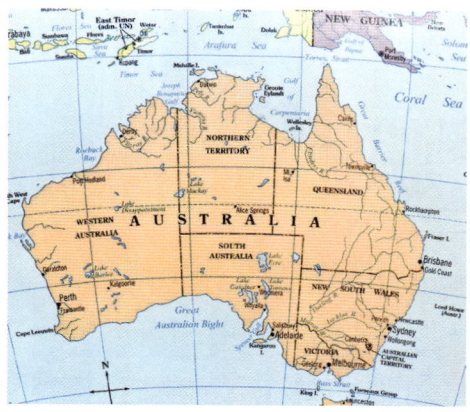

It's a living thing, and you can see it from space. What is it?

It's the Great Barrier Reef. It's 2,600 kilometers long, and it's the world's largest **coral** reef – and coral is a living thing.

People like to visit the reef. They go there to swim and to see the bright colors of the coral and the fish, and the many different kinds of birds. However, the reef is in danger. The sea is getting warmer, and sometimes the coral turns white and dies. Fishing can also be a problem. You can't fish at all on one third of the reef. And on the other two thirds, you can only fish at special times.

Video Quest

The Great Barrier Reef

Watch this video about the Great Barrier Reef. How many different reefs are there?

Think of Australian animals. Here are two popular ones – the kangaroo and the koala.

Their babies are born very small and weak. Then the mother carries them for some time in a pouch. They can get milk inside the pouch. This type of animal is called a **marsupial**.

Not all marsupials live in Australia. The opossum, for example, is a marsupial that lives in North America. Marsupials moved to North America about 100 million years ago. At that time, Australia, Antarctica, and South America were all together in one big continent called Gondwana. The marsupials traveled through South America and Antarctica and arrived in Australia about 60 million years later. Of course, those marsupials were probably not like the kangaroo and the koala we know today. Animals change a lot over millions of years.

A kangaroo carries her baby in a pouch.

A koala

An opossum

The first Australians, the Aborigines, arrived thousands of years ago, maybe 50,000 years ago. They came from the north, through the Indonesian islands.

Year after year they moved across Australia. They never met any other people until 1788, when the first Europeans arrived. After this, more and more Europeans came to Australia. They took the land and they killed many Aborigines. Other Aborigines died from the diseases[6] that the new people brought with them.

In 1933 there were only 74,000 Aborigines left, maybe a quarter of the number there were in 1788. Life is better now, but still difficult for Australia's first people.

But even today, when people think of Australia, they often think of Aborigines. They think of their dances and their music played on the didgeridoo. And they think of their art – dot paintings.

He's playing a didgeridoo.

[6]**disease:** a sickness

? ANALYZE

Living in the same country with another people is sometimes difficult. Can you think of other countries where "old" and "new" people live well or not so well together?

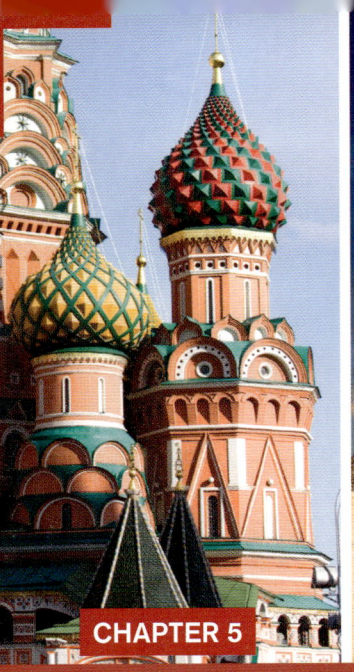  

CHAPTER 5

What Do You Think?

In this book we read about the people and things that describe these places:

- a city: Moscow – onion domes, ushanka hats, caviar

- a country: Egypt – the River Nile, pyramids, cotton

- a continent: Australia – the Great Barrier Reef, marsupials, Aborigines

What did you learn about these people, animals, places, and things?

Which one did you most enjoy reading about? Which place – Moscow, Egypt, or Australia – would you most like to visit? Why?

Where do you live? What things do you think of when you think about the town or city you live in? About the country you live in? And about your continent? Think of three things for each place.

Think about things like these:

- a building, or type of building

- a type of food

- a type of car, motorcycle, bus, tram, train, etc.

- a sport

- something to wear

- a popular place for visitors

- something that people buy

- an animal

- people

After You Read

Choose Ⓐ (True) or Ⓑ (False). If the book does not tell you, choose Ⓒ (Doesn't say).

1 Many bagels are eaten in New York City for breakfast.

Ⓐ True
Ⓑ False
Ⓒ Doesn't say

2 American mail workers wear ushankas.

Ⓐ True
Ⓑ False
Ⓒ Doesn't say

3 Today, very little caviar comes from the Caspian Sea.

Ⓐ True
Ⓑ False
Ⓒ Doesn't say

4 Ancient Egyptians built pyramids for their pharaohs.

Ⓐ True
Ⓑ False
Ⓒ Doesn't say

5 Most pyramids are east of the Nile.

Ⓐ True
Ⓑ False
Ⓒ Doesn't say

6 Egypt grows more cotton than any other country.

Ⓐ True
Ⓑ False
Ⓒ Doesn't say

7 Sydney is the capital of Australia.

   Ⓐ True

   Ⓑ False

   Ⓒ Doesn't say

8 In the near future, no one will fish on the Great Barrier Reef.

   Ⓐ True

   Ⓑ False

   Ⓒ Doesn't say

9 Marsupials only live in Australia.

   Ⓐ True

   Ⓑ False

   Ⓒ Doesn't say

Find the Answers

Write one word, name, or number on each line.

1 Caviar comes from this fish.

_____

2 Most caviar comes from this sea.

_____

3 The biggest pyramids are here.

_____

4 This is the number of countries the Nile flows through, including Egypt.

_____

5 A marsupial mother carries her young in this.

_____

6 Aborigines play music on this.

_____

Answer Key

Words to Know, page 4
Moscow: **1** domes **2** fur **3** War

Words to Know, page 5
Egypt: **1** pryamids **2** flood **3** cotton
Australia: **1** Great Barrier Reef **2** coral **3** marsupials

New York, page 6
1 A **2** B **3** C

Geography, page 7
1 Antarctica **2** Africa **3** South America

Video Quest, page 9
Communism ended in Russia in 1991.

Evaluate, page 11   *Answers will vary.*

Video Quest, page 13
The pyramids are older.

Analyze, page 15   *Answers will vary.*

Video Quest, page 17
Three thousand separate reefs make up the Great Barrier Reef.

Analyze, page 19   *Answers will vary.*

True or False?, page 22
1 A **2** A **3** B **4** A **5** B **6** C **7** B **8** C **9** B

Find the Answers, page 23
1 sturgeon **2** Caspian **3** Giza **4** nine **5** pouch
6 didgeridoo